BENZIE BEE AND THE ALPHABETS

BY: BERNETTA W. FARMER

LIFE'S GOLDEN TRINKETS PUBLICATIONS

My name is Benzie Bumble Bee!
I'll tell you why I'm here.

We'll together learn the Alphabet
and put a buzz in your ear!

This is my big helper
Her name is Blaney Bee!

Our goal is to encourage you!

Please listen while we speak.

3

WE WILL START WITH THE FIRST LETTER IN THE
ALPHABET AND CONTINUE TO THE END.

4

NOW THAT WE'VE GOT YOUR ATTENTION

We will now begin!

A is for the awesome person that you are!
B is for be the best you can be and you will surely go far!

C is for courage to stand for what is right.

D is for doing your best and trying with all your might!

E is for encourage yourself and you will surely grow.

F is for funtastic so enjoy the life you know!

G is for get ready to put a smile on someone's face.

H is for how happy you can make a person today!

I is for **inside** of you lies a golden key, that unlocks the door to smiles for everyone to see!

J will bring you full of joy to share with all the world!

K is for the kind heart inside every boy and girl!

L is for the love you spread to everyone you meet!

M is for making each day count to move forward and succeed!

N is for *never* give up on

yourself this you cannot ignore.

O is for *opportunities* knocking

at your door.

14

P is for **positive** learning what life has to offer you!

Q is for the **quiet** time you'll need to muddle through.

R is for the road you choose
when a choice has to be made.

S is for you're a shining star,
stay focused and concentrate!

T is for the time you cherish every moment of your life.

U is for understanding who you Are and no one can take that spot light!

V is for **victory** stand for what is brave and true!

W is for **wisdom** that will always guide you through and through!

X is for the xtraordinary places you will go!

Y is for young at heart stay pure and you will grow.

Z is for zesty personality that others will soon meet!

Now together we've learned the alphabet from the letter **A** all the way to **Z!**

Life's Golden Trinket – Learning
encourages your mind and Reading
encourages your heart!

BENZIE BEE AND THE ALPHABETS

LEARNING ENCOURAGES YOUR MIND AND READING ENCOURAGES YOUR HEART.

Published by: Life's Golden Trinkets Publications

Life's Golden Trinkets Publications
7399 Shadeland Ave.
STE #137
Indianapolis, IN 46250

BENZIE BEE AND THE ALPHABETS
978-0-9893245-4-0

www.ingramcontent.com/pod-product-compliance
Lightning Source LLC
Chambersburg PA
CBHW042119040426
42449CB00002B/102